Hi, I am Shana Smi
I am a wife, and a m
proud Philly girl wi
travel but my first love has always
reside in Virginia Beach, Virginia.

I love 90 sitcoms!

One of my favorite tv shows to watch from the 90s is a show called A Different World. There's an episode where Professor Jordan, who is played by the actress Whoopi Goldberg, tells Tisha Campbell's character that she is a voice in this world and she deserves to be heard. The students are given an assignment where they have to create their eulogies and share them with their classmates. Josie, who is played by Tisha, wants to reveal that she has Acquired Immune Deficiency Syndrome (AIDS) during her presentation. She hopes that by sharing her story she could encourage her classmates to practice safe sex but is afraid of how her peers are going to respond. Nevertheless, she decides to go forward with her truth anyway.

As a teen, I could relate to Josie. I found it difficult to tell my truth. Often holding onto trauma, pain, and family secrets that plagued me. I desired to release what I was dealing with but the few times I did let friends or family in I ended up getting hurt so I quickly learned how to stay quiet.

However, writing poetry made me brave. It gave me space to scream, cry, ask questions, and even dream. As a teen, I used poetry as my therapy. Poetry helped me process my emotions.

Now as an adult, I use my words to challenge the norms, cultivate awareness, activate solutions, and encourage my students to tell their stories. Still, there are moments when I question if people even care about what I have to say. That is when I hear Professor Jordan say "You are a voice in this world and deserve to be heard" and I tell myself "Yes I am!"

Anyway, back to you.
Thank you for choosing to go on this journey with me.

I hope you feel seen between these pages.
I hope my poetry comforts you, encourages you, and allows you moments to exhale and even grieve.
Most importantly, I hope you know that you are not alone in this gigantic world full of enchantment and chaos.
I am walking with you.
It is our experiences, both marvelous and dreadful that keep us connected.

This bit of me was always intended for us.

Chapter 1: Agape

Sundays

Sundays feel love-sick,
like waking up to cuddles on his side of the king,
like listening to Maverick City while folding crispy sheets.
Lingers on my breath like shrimp and grits and a tall glass of mimosa.

Sundays feel like the fresh breeze of weed coming from my neighbor's crib,
warm bubble baths and black cherry candles,
like sushi picnics eaten at the foot of the bed with Bae.

Sundays feel like a long walk on a Puerto Vallarta beach,
an unexpected visit from my Cali sis,
hot mint tea before nightfall.

Sundays feel like oversized hoodies on a chilly November day,
a tiny nap and a swift daydream,
like hubby's strong hands caressing my waist.

Yeah, Sundays
feel like home
to me.

Full

These vibes,
this place,
his energy.

My dimples,
his voice,
that smile.

Those butterflies,
my heartbeat,
his reach.

His smell,
that crease,
our laughter.

My breath,
his hands,
the possibilities.

This pleasure,
our joy,
that magic.

Our kids,
this home,
His glory

Those fights,
that bitterness,
our pain.

This grace,
our growth,
new memories.

His patience,
my healing,
those trips.

This journey,
our love,
my God,

repeat.

Wonderfully Made

My body carries warmth like the sun.
I claim her sweet like a watermelon smoothie
in the Costa Rican shade.

My body is not meant just to gratify

but to yield.

Humans cannot sit in judgment of my body.
It belongs to no man but is molded by He who holds everything.

My body is not a makeshift target.
It is not a place for hood dudes in loud cars to shoot their shots off of.

My body has rolls that protrude from my tummy.
breasts that spread like rumors after the bra is undone,
marks that no longer easily fade but remind me that I carried two miracles.

My body is designed to soothe,
to nurture,
to offer rest on wretched days.

Labors long just to come home
and work some more.
My body feels guilty for asking for time off
but knows that she deserves it.

Sinful yet still a sanctuary.
My body carries heartbreak.
Knows how to forgive even if it's not instant.

My body is a blessing.
a wake-up call
has always been Earth's remedy.

Sweet Tea Kisses
(In memory of my Great Grandma Sallie)

It's in her sweet tea tongue.
Her shady side-eye stares.
The way she comforts and confronts
with the same twang.

It's in her rich chocolate skin.
The flow of her wavy ebony hair.
How's she hates taking pictures
but the lens longs for her smile.

It's in her fragrant hugs.
The scent of lavender and coffee lingers.
The warmth of arms wrapped tight.
Where home and freedom are found.

It's in her gentle laughter.
The way she speaks with her whole face.
Each inflection is perfected by God above, and
even when she says just a few words everyone holds their
breath.

It's in her homemade quilt.
The stitching is reminiscent of tree-lined canals in Augusta.
A reminder of a life well-traveled.
Each patch tells its own story.
How delicate hands scrubbed floors
so I could earn degrees.

It's in her selflessness.
Pack of Winston's on the nightstand.
The smell of Listerine on the bathroom sink.
Homemade biscuits were made fresh each morning.
The ones she never taught us how to make
because this is how a grandma shows she cares.

It's in her morning glow.
Nightly reminders to not burn her electricity.
Saturdays were full of Night Rider, MacGyver, and A-Team.
Thirty-cent was placed in my third-grade hands for a soft pretzel.
Sneaking pieces of crispy pork to me behind Mama's back.

It's in the way she called me Shiny and never Shana.
How she saw my inner light long before I was able to flip the switch for myself.

How she never judged me for my softness,
took her time to nurture my gifts,
made me feel seen.

It's in how she lifted,
how she lived,
how she left,
waiting for me.

Me and my great-grandmother Sallie Ross after I came home to visit from college.

Philly Tongue
(After E'Mon Lauren "Speak")

They say I have an accent,
but what they hear is the corner of 20th and Parrish.
I have a ghetto in my twang.

North Philly slang drips from my mouth.
I keep a "you tried it" on my lips
and a "you drawing" floating in the back of my throat.

I speak second-born child,
overlooked and blended in.
I have no regard for runner-ups
because I've lived there most of my life.

I speak hand me downs
and House of Bargains,
converses and cardigans,
humbling potholes on-95,
girl fights and Vaseline.

Grandma Sallie taught me about cheese eggs and generosity.
I speak empathy and Augusta.
I speak homemade,
struggle,
homelessness and gurgling guts,
house parties and Moscato,
Joel Embiid and Jalen Hurts.
I speak not knowing how it feels to win a championship till you actually win one.

I speak cheesesteaks and Cafe Soho wings.
Some of the best damn food you'll ever eat.

Mira Mira snaps my neck,
so I speak Papi stores and penny candy,
summer sun on south street,
Fresh Prince and Jill Scott.
Soul clings to me like a wet tee shirt.

I hear never forget where you came from, so don't come for me.
Mama's mac and cheese rests on my hips.
Daddy's hustle is embedded in my walk.
My sister's sass is delivered when I spit.

I speak teenage mother
and grown kids.

I speak Philly.
I speak free Meek.
On the corner where they sell water ice and soft pretzels.

I speak Broad Street bully,
Germantown gutter,
southwest stick up boys,
the gentrified Garden.
Cold winters and harsh summers
all on them Septa buses.

So when they ask me where I'm from
I speak.

11

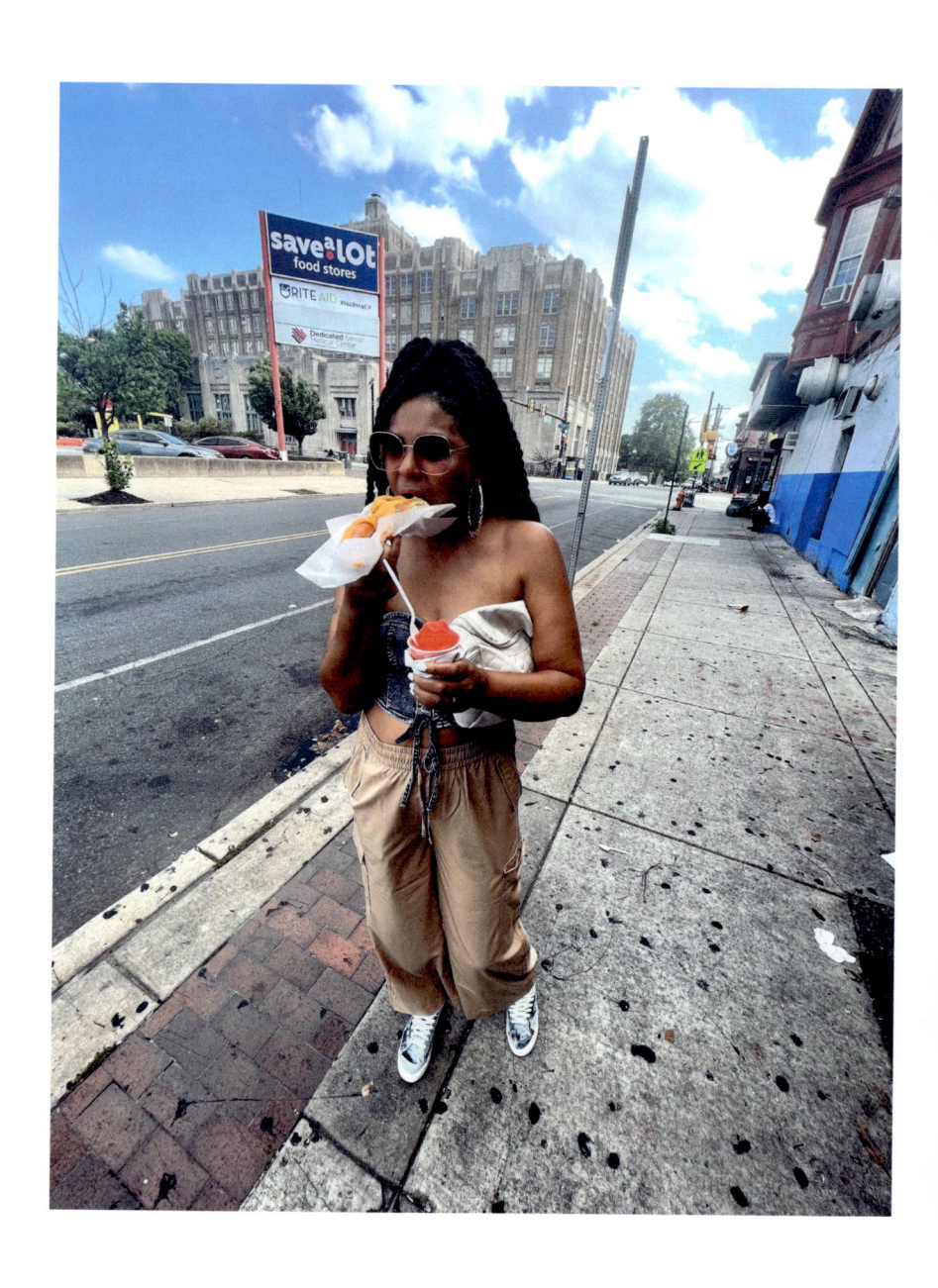

An Ode To The Black Crayon

I met your scribble in my coloring book long before I knew your nature.
Watch you highlight and confiscate with the same rhythm.

Always there to fix my flaws black crayon, you turned mistakes into magic long before David Copperfield.
Permitted me to live in my Ariel until I was able to accept my Halle Bailey.

Still, I would break you into pieces.
Pushing you down with gripped fingers to get each outline just right.
It's funny how the most dependable ones often get overused.
Not recognizing that the gift was in your possibilities, never your perfection.

Now that I'm wiser, I realize how worn out you must be.
Often described as the absence of color because you gave yours all away.
Nevertheless, no amount of church, I mean tape could fix you,
so you learned to function unwrapped.

Still, I'm sorry that I never said thank you.
I never acknowledged the courage behind your smile.

You are more than just some marks on a preschooler's paper.
More than a toddler writing utensil, or chewing toy.

You are power in a little girl's hands.

Lending your influence to her style and confidence.
Reminding Black women that it's okay to be boss and a beauty.
That it's okay to be the anchor in your community when resources start to drift.

It's okay to even break.
To know that a strong friend sometimes becomes the weak one.

It's okay to take a risk.
To splatter your tint all across this here white canvas and know that you,
I,
and her,
We were all created to be art.

Black Joy

Yesterday my hubby sent me a video on Instagram that made pools of water rush free from my eyes.
The thing is there was no traffic stop gone wrong.
no child went missing,
no women being victimized,
no bullets, collapsing bodies,
or chaos in a waffle house.
Just a comedian spreading joy in a grocery store,
so I wrote this poem.

Black Joy be bold and alive.
Black Joy is laughing until the tears flow,
laughing until the ribs crack,
laughing until the dirt on the floor knows your curves by name.

It is having stiff drinks with real friends to celebrate all that real work you put in all week.

Black Joy is roller skating backward with the music bouncing in your feet
It is last-minute date nights sporting matching 1s with bae.
It is throwing over-the-top birthday parties that your children won't remember.

Black Joy is open mics that turn into praise sessions.
It's eclectic art and funky style.
It is bun baring beach days
It's getting on a flight and smiling at every girl you see with braids.

Black Joy is turning a hobby into a purpose,
a gathering into a ministry,
a hustle into a legacy.

Black Joy is
singing with a church choir stuck deep within your throat.
It is rooting for everyone that's Black.
Supporting your Black friends.
Buying T-shirts with all the Black sayings.

Black Joy is color-coordinated events with no concept of time.
Tiny Desks covered in Tank and the Bangas and Durand Bernarr.
It is comedy shows and poetry slams.
It is Grandma's wisdom and Grandpa's humor.

Black Joy is turning rest into a revolution.
It's being seen and fully accepted.
It is loud sisterly support and
brave brotherly vulnerability.

Black Joy is luminous.
It shifts spirits,
it breaks strongholds,
it calms fears,
its repairs the broken,
it is sustainable and inspiring,
intoxicating and unwavering.

Black Joy is,

what it is,
cause it is,
us.

When My Other Half Is Missing

My bed tells me I'm different when you're gone.
Calls me out for my unruly disposition.
Says my fidgeting and fumbling have become too toxic.
Doesn't understand why I need the light from the screen to rock me to sleep
when his organic coziness is abundantly available.

I try to convince him that it's me, not him.
That it's unfair to compete with over a decade of bonding.
Still, he sees how my frame drops worries in your presence.
Eyes that once fought to stay open now take pleasure in the ease of letting go.
No need for a nightlight when even your dreams know their way around my darkness.
I'm not sure when my body stopped learning how to rest without you.
I just know that my spirit has a way of letting me know when my other half is missing.

Retreat

There are days when I marinate on pause.
Allowing the breeze of guilt to hit my cheek. Unable to give that which some may seek.
Days where I don't feel like mothering, cleaning, or collecting other people's catastrophes.
This calm I promise I'm keeping for myself.
Tucked beneath this blanket along with my head.
Still, the rays that peek through beckon motivation.
I don't move.
I am lost in a pivot of placement.
Centered in the abyss of comfort.
Reminded that it's not lazy to love myself.
That it's not selfish to take what I need,
to surrender to stillness in a time when everything around me is pleading for my attention.
I cover my head and find the courage to retreat.

18

Be a Bloom

Be a bloom.
Go where shallow water leads
crooked and untapped
even if no one shows you how to grow.

So I chipped pieces of me.
I caught thorns beneath my teeth.
Watched as the forest stood still while I grew sideways.

The wind blew echoes of my worth like fall leaves.
Had me thinking, who am I to believe a weed like me belongs
in my Father's garden?

Be a bloom they said.

Light made me see myself.
Sacred tears exposed my stains.
Grace gave healing to my roots, and
hope to my weary leaves.
I collected chances and called them second.

Be a bloom they said.

That's when I stopped competing with other blossoms.
Abba reminded me that I am where the sun goes to shine.

Unbow your head, sweet daughter.
Shame has no place on a flower's face.

So I rise,
I wake,
I fall,
I bloom,
I am blooming,
I say.

Joy-full

Meeting joy feels different.
Hugs compress back full and deliberate.
No forced dimples or fake exchanges.
Teeth claim lips as they pose to.
Laughter becomes intoxicating.
Kindness darts through wounded hearts like a cure.
It's witnessing Johovah's warmth in human form.
Therefore, I find jars of mason to catch the glimmer in.
In hopes that one day I might inhale and become joy-full too.

Me and my sister from another mister. Karla Sharee. She is one of the most joy-full human beings I've ever met!

Chapter 2: Expectation

Loyalty

I wish loyalty poured heavily like concrete.
That it didn't cost my roots trauma
to plant my secrets.

I wish that when harm threatens to come my way my body set
off vapors to reject it.

That my conscious self
was better at separating ego from the offense,
and my tongue was better at building boundaries than talking
greasy.

I wish my thoughts didn't make it so arduous
to trust new people,
and my winter didn't have
such a hold on my spring.

That my brokenness didn't teach me
how to treat you,
instead, I learned by listening to your heartbeat,
because I'm getting too old
to keep learning how to fly over and over again.

Renewed

Yesterday's heartbreak feels incomplete.

Like chewing on a loss I have not made room to swallow.

I caught a glimpse of my grief in my rearview but cut her off

before she got too close

because Black women don't have time to weep.

Instead, I washed myself with the tears I

dropped in the shower

and called myself renewed.

Bittersweet

If I have mastered anything it's the way my soul feels when I breathe hope into it.
Living, although not easy, comes with extraordinary possibilities.

I've tasted melancholy long before I tasted ice cream.
Milk from my mother's breast wasn't sweet enough to make my salty childhood memories disappear.

I've sifted through the shame that didn't belong to me.
Carried burdens around like 10-pound babies,
too heavy for this small frame.
Too many times I've cried myself to sleep
weighing my sins against my sacrifices.

I don't like trauma
but I swear she left her stench on me.
Spread her pessimism across my sheets,
then covered me up in insecurities.

I scrubbed my bed with a hyssop.
My spirit is now at least halfway clean.
Made peace with imperfections.

Told Satan he couldn't have my joy, my mind, or my motivation.
Told men that didn't match my magic they could not stay.
No time for fake friends,

I like these four well enough.

On this journey, I've seen God through the cocoa eyes of those that once bathed in my womb.
Caught a contact high with my first passport stamp.
Set a match to every memory that made me feel unworthy.
Laid my buns bare in the crystal waters of the Cayman.

I know it's easy to stay mad at the world for what you think it owes you,
but I'd rather ride the rollercoaster with my hands extended to the clouds,
slow kiss the man that makes my heart skip a beat,
drink Moscato on weekends while binging on Netflix.

I know the rain will come
and unfortunately, some days taste more bitter than they do sweet.
Still, have you ever licked the sauce from Cafe Soho wings off your fingers?
Danced to Marley in a room full of Chicago strangers?
Hit the pause button on a long day just to get high off a sunset?
You see I've consumed more heaven than hell already.

So no worries to the guy that cut me off on my way to work this morning.
I forgave you before the light turned green.

The Nappy Truth

From God's hand through momma's hips
I enter a distorted place.
One where a glowy box of hair tamer is delivered even before
a tampon.

In this galaxy,
Black mothers lay out flat irons and Blue Magic to
commemorate this day.
Tell me "You be pretty now!"

Because nothing says African American more than sweet
potato pie and straight hair,
and us Black girls are supposed to eat them both.

Gobble them up
like fat boys eat cake.

Let perms burn blisters onto our scalps
and call them relaxers.

But what if one day my appetite changes?
I choose my naps over Westernized beauty.
Tie ribbons around my kinks and call this day my birthday.

I don't tell momma.
I let her discover this planet with fresh eyes as I did.

One where Black girls rock their afros on purpose.
Coils so deep, rich & chocolate they spring from Augusta dirt
like Grandma Ba.

On this land, I'll pledge allegiance to my flag.
Tell corporate America that these curls are not up for negotiation.
Tell momma I stopped believing in her kind of freedom a long time ago.

She sees me as a cyborg now.
Sometimes it seems artificial to others
when you start to treasure
your gold.

Although my name means God is gracious
She fails to recognize that He made this garden too.
Every strand picked perfectly in his sight.
Strong enough to go with the fire He placed inside of me.

Yet all Mama sees is smoke.
Clouded by the lies they force-fed our ancestors.
Without knowing she ate and got full.

So she asks me "Daughter when will you return?"

I reply,
I already have.

28

Voting Season

I don't know much about politics
but I see two parties that brawl like Tyson and Holyfield.
Enormous egos ignoring the needs of the hearts they swore to keep beating.

Presidential debates look more like sandbox quarrels than a discussion about the issues.
Spreading division around like COvID-19.
Going from "Yes We Can" to "How did we get here?"
Is my sister still my sister if she hashtags all lives matter
but doesn't ask me if I'm okay?

I don't know much about politics,
but I know the system that I'm sifting through ain't just.
Systematic oppression bears its ugly head like a cockroach at a cocktail party.
My timeline is saturated with too many innocent bodies that resemble me.
While dirty cops get a slap on the wrist and a pension in their pocket.
It's getting arduous to teach our youth how to rock their crown in a world that doesn't see their ebony skin as worthy.

I don't know much about politics,
but I know kids that avoid bullets like dodgeballs.
Too scared to walk home from school alone so they avoid education altogether.
Underpaid teachers create curriculums with handcuffs on.
I guess it's easy to lose your passion when those in charge won't let you use it.

I once heard nothing stops a bullet like a job, so where are they in my community?
City leaders see our neighborhoods as gutters so they treat us like garbage.
Unwilling to recognize the dazzling sunflowers sprouting beneath their noses so they push to build something artificial instead.

The real looters are still at work.
Taking what they desire and disposing of the people that once called this land their home.

I don't know much about politics.
Still, this offense that I'm carrying is weighing me down.
Strapping cinder blocks to a body that was designed to fly.

Politics got me looking at old friends like new enemies.
A country divided is a family torn, but I remember how it felt to break bread together.
To have differences without disconnecting.
Surely, hands that build bridges can find their way back there.

I have faith in a nation that looks more like a box of Crayola than a pack of number two pencils.
Maybe it was never about politics
but the people that created them.

31

Brown Boy

Dear brown boy, you were birthed out of tragedy,
yet you still beam.
Oh, how brilliant is your audacity?

Colorless

Imagine a world void of color.
Snatched away like an unkept promise.
No luminous light to greet each morning.

Every item in your closet is now a boring batch of fabric.
Button-ups are just as bitter as your graphics tees.

Every egg scrambled a twin to the bacon and the plate.
Makes your taste buds feel temporary.

Flowers have no rhythm,
birds sing no melody,
clouds offer little make-believe,
no blues to paint your sadness.

A world where there is no melanin attached to the skin.
Each of us is a reminder of our true selves,
both flawed and fabulous.
Recognized by our humanity and not the fullness of our pockets.

Spit now swallowed.
School floors only know the thump of colorless feet.
Fountains drunk from every mouth.
Books welcome hands that want to read not just those allowed to.
All beaches are now a haven.
Every bus ride is a smooth transition.

Blacks are not labeled as three-fifths human

because what is Black?

Crosses no longer burned on lawns,
the N-word was never spray-painted on homes,
and Travon and his hood are never labeled as a threat.

Just a kid walking home with a pack of uninteresting taste the rainbows in his pocket.
Just a kid
walking home
with a pack of uninteresting taste the rainbows in his pocket.

White men aren't seen as devils
because who is White?

Bonds are now formed out of missions, not greed.
Systems are now curated out of love not power.

Is the lack of hue worth the gain of freedom?
Could man make room for a space more virtuous than religious?

Laura Titus

(In response to Laura Titus being the first woman to discover the YWCA)

I'm used to being stolen from.
Watched others pick my petals and call themselves the flower.

It's funny how black pearls are never really treasured until they're found in whitewashed hands.

How easily we go missing and no one comes to find us, until we search the pages to find ourselves.

Tell the stories they thought they buried with their bigotry.
Let Laura Titus's name fall first from their lips for a chance.

Her mission is a fact, not a theory.
Like Catherine Johnson, she too was a hidden figure,
so we reclaim her rightful place on the throne.

Placing a crown of appreciation on her head.
No longer just a woman on assignment
but the art we hold in our hands.
The poems we reach for with our hearts.
The gentle wings of a vision we take flight on.

Beneath the Shadows
(A response piece to the Kara Walker exhibit at the Museum of Contemporary Art in Virginia Beach)

My great-grandmother once told me that darkness and light cannot coexist without shadows.
This is where they go to bury the truth, she said.

Four hundred years later and the road to freedom is still blocked.

Exchanging false bottom wagons for coffins and coach bags.
This is for those of us who know we are the walking dead and alive all at the same time.

How does a Black man reach his destination when random traffic stops turn into modern-day lynchings?

We are told to silence our grief.
To remove the calliope that disturbs their children's harmony.

Dear America
I regret to inform you that banning books doesn't make our stories less relevant,
suspending officers doesn't make this threat to my skin less critical.

We hold this truth to be self-evident that communities of color still grapple with slave systems etched in our backs.

Each lash is a reminder of underpaid wages and overworked bodies,
mass incarcerations and school-to-prison pipelines.

Do you know what it means to have a wound that never heals? -Natasha Trethewey
How it festers and trickles through your bloodline like a disease.
Contaminating progress and dismantling legacy.

Never forget the Tulsa Oklahoma race massacre.
Colonizers have always been afraid of mass production they can't control,
so they resort to mass shootings.
Leaving a trail of melanated bodies from the churches of Charleston South Carolina to the grocery stores in Buffalo.

Do you ever wonder why funeral processions look like a parade?
Cause there's always somebody, somewhere celebrating.

Nevertheless, there's a Black mother somewhere ready to forgive no matter how tragic her loss.

Let us not be a nation that adorns wooden boxes with flowers as an attempt to cover the stink of the truth.

Rather a people
more like our youth.
That once told me in order to keep a plant in place I must first learn to respect its roots.

Relief
(This piece was written during the COVID-19 lockdown)

How hollow is the well we take ownership of?
Not knowing that at any moment it could be lost.

Blown away by the breath of the universe,
crushed by its melancholy.

Moonlight keeps shadows but darkness owns no light.

Nor does a man own wine.
These grapes belong to the earth
and so shall they return.

Treat me now unto the sun.
I'll find my way back.

Beyond the layers of provision lost.
Beyond the leaders that failed their flock.
Beyond the bodies that once held space
now rest in new homes.

For bridges do not know who shall cross them.
Just that one might in order to get to the other side.

So we create.
Chasing down enchanted rainbows.
Crashing streams against dry land.
For the community is our cornerstone.
Piercing every metal anchor.

Flight is near.

Dawn has risen.

Wisdom is bound.

Relief is but a stretch away for arms that crave a new day.

Chapter 3: Surrender

We Matter

The first time my heart grieved for a man I did not know was
when I saw the video of Philando Castille taking his last breaths,
as Diamond Reynold's screamed for his life with a baby in the back seat.

Screamed for her love,
screamed for a second chance at being Black and safe,
screamed for her family to ride off, go home, eat dinner, and be safe,
get ready for work the next morning
and be whole,
and safe.

Be a father to her baby,
a lunch man to the kids at the school where he worked, and was admired,
and was safe,
and whole.

Instead, police splashed Philando's blood all over the front car seat
and neither he,
nor Diamond,

or baby,
made it home whole, or safe,
just broken.

That's when I caught myself at 700 East Olney Road, in a seventeen by twenty-foot room, in the middle of a poetry workshop, where I was supposed to be teaching little brown kids poetry, not points on how they have to be twice as educated as those Ghent kids.

Even then they may not make it home safe or whole,
but at least they might have a chance.

I screamed as they watched.
Tears poured from my brown eyes like fresh springs.
Asking for answers they could not give me.
Falling apart in a room full of children who I'm supposed to catch,
somehow ended up catching me.

Watched me,
the lead teaching artist at their home away from home sobbing through each word as she preached.

Somehow when you try to tell a group of teens how to avoid dying by those that swore to protect them when you really don't know yourself, it all just seems to come out like a sermon,
a sign of faith,

because you want to believe in justice as much as you do
Christ, but God is more tangible.

So you hope that your words,
these screams,
this pain
that shoots out like lava
           will not be in vain.

That Philandos death
           will not be in vain.

That Diamond Reynold's Heartbreak
           will not be in vain.

That this video you've seen replay time and time again of an innocent Black man being killed
who you know could have been your brother,
                    son,
                    or friend
        will not be in vain.

Then you realize maybe this pain isn't new.
Maybe it's just the first time you've seen it let loose from your body.
Perhaps your body has been dragging these chains around all along.

That this raw conversation you're having with these amazing young people,
           will not be in vain.

43

So you catch your breath,
wipe your tears
and wonder...
Did I even say enough?

This photo was taken at a protest I participated in four days after Philando Castile was killed.

Boss Of The Block

One thing North Philly has a lot of are stray cats.
As a kid, I often wondered why our streets litter cats like empty soda cans.
Each one carries more lives than nine.

It's not their fault that the same ones that welcomed them in,
kicked them out with pure resentment.

It must be difficult to be abandoned after being loved.
Nevertheless, stray cat you scratch on.

Clawing your way through every alley.
Sleeping beneath warm cars to beat the brick.
Outrunning the boy next door that tries to set fire to your tail.

You be as cunning as you are conceited.
Chasing down mice for a hearty meal or a playful toy.
Willing to accept the charity of humans but unlike dogs won't beg for it.

I think that's why I dislike and admire you all at the same time.
You were born with built-in confidence.
Never needing a man to like your post...I mean purr

You be the savage beast of Allegheny.
Nothing like the pussy they labeled you.

These Tears

I'm tired of the need for growth coming in one song.
The same verse repeated with no melody.
Flowers were never meant to just rest on graves but to be held in hands.

Feels like I've been planting seeds into concrete instead of community.
Hoping that a rose will immerse but all I keep getting are weeds.

When the gun fires
an emptiness fills my gut again.
Vomiting from this pill they've forced me to swallow
and only time can ease this pain.

A few blocks away from the garden
three mothers bleed out in front of their children.
Don't know them but I've played a costar in this horror film before
and it seems like the boogie man is winning.

These tears fall on fresh ground as if the pavement ordered them.
Have seen much yet shift for gratitude like they do grief.

These tears take refuge in me.
Claim my insides like a baby's first heartbeat.
Effortlessly sweet.

These tears ask for help when mouths can't.

You spot them in the neighborhood bully,
watch them nodding off by the BP,
catch glimpses in the teenage girl that pops too many pills on purpose.

These tears are pallbearers and still look for vengeance.
Nevertheless, I have hope for them.
I see their potential when the mirror gets blurry.
Watch them produce a harvest in places that once set dry.

These tears come from warriors and worriers.
Tell me Shana you can't save everybody
but I ain't never been good at quitting!

Wide Tooth

After Audre Lord,
To the ones who've paused,
Held in an exhausted breath.
Combed their hair with the words their White friends never spoke.

Their silence became a wide tooth.
Exposing the ebony and ivory flesh of what used to be our gray.

To the ones who packed their gut with patience,
but still couldn't stomach smiling Instagram pictures or every day as a usual Facebook post.
While the murders of George Floyd and Brionna Taylor walk free.

Hoping to feel the warmth of a Black Live Matters song dripping from your lips,
but the melody never played.
The sun never left your mouth.

Saw videos of brown bodies pleading with last breath
but you stay unbothered.
Speaking about the looting but never the real looters.

Strolling past our pain like it's just another walk in the park.
While grief pulls us to our knees,
makes us revisit the trauma we tucked away with the loose change,

turns our sobs into protest signs,
demands that we teach our melanated babies how to submit before the submission is even necessary.

But how do you teach a boy or girl to be on guard in their own home?
You remind them that they're Black.
When your skin is dark like coffee in America, catching a peaceful sleep is a gift, not a requirement.

To those that call me sister, yet step over my contorted flesh like a Pharisee,
Is it possible to sip Christian tea between your lips but swallow no empathy?

Wondering how you've known me for all these years but never saw me at all.
Never learned to appreciate the parts of me that make you uncomfortable.

Willing to trade in all this magic for that make-believe.
Calling America the greatest feels like hot grease thrown in my face.
I can't even kneel at a football game without being punted away.

While others run up capital steps with Confederate flags.
Kill cops and make it home to brag about it.

Oh, how different freedom is for those that came here by choice
and those whose ancestors came here in cages.

20th Street

20-year-old me
dripping crop top
and frayed shorts.

He sits close.
Close enough to smell Issey Miyake
on toasted chestnut skin.

Caesar cut to perfection.
Skittles play hopscotch on boys' tongues.

Never seen my friend like this before.
The way a toddler looks at strawberries after the first bite.

Now I too want to taste
the rainbow.

Let him wear out my tongue with his sweetness.
Run urgent through my mouth like a refugee.

His lips
remind me of safety.
Feels like the last stop on the subway after a long day.
Makes me forget I got daddy issues.
Calms me like hot tea.
The kind grandma gives to soothe a sore throat.

Maybe I'm still sick
cause my friend got my skin clammy.
Has my heart pounding like a drum line.
I see majorettes in the distance.

I imagine myself wearing him
like my favorite leotard,
snug and complete.

Yes, we become warm and familiar.
Like sweet potato pie and Cool Whip,
like hurricanes and rainbows,
like a seesaw with your favorite cousin.

On this North Philly Block,
in this three-story home,
on my mother's peach sofa,
on 20th Street.

Dislocation

Usually self-diagnosable,
Symptoms include out-of-place behavior, swelling of anger,
pain due to trauma, and lack of support. Causing an inability
to move forward in life.
A dislocation.

I know single moms that lay feet to grind all day just to keep
the lights on.
Baby daddies can't stay out of orange jumpsuits long enough
to pay attention
so child support becomes nonexistent.

I know Black women that strap book bags to middle-aged
backs hoping to get that education they sacrificed for their
children.

I know brown girls whose legs swing open like double doors
for dudes that didn't deserve their dimensions.
They label her a thot.
Body built for their lust, but never for their loyalty.

They never ask why the brown girl is the way she is.
Maybe innocence got ripped out from under her like slaves
from their homeland,
or maybe she never knew what it felt like to be treasured by
her dad so she settled for fools gold instead.

They never ask why big girl fights.
Why she's quick to throw hands instead of using her words?
Why sis anger turns from zero to a hundred like Solange
kicks in that elevator?

Maybe she's walked away from bullies for far too long.
Saw Mama get black eyes from dudes that claim to adore her,
but wasn't told enough to stop them,
so now this rage that she holds onto falls fiercely on the first
person with a slick tongue.
It's not her fault.
She's been groomed to live a lifestyle where violence is the
only way to get your attention.

This is how Black Girl cries.
Our truth leaves lips free,
yet comes back hostile.
Get shredded apart by the opinions of others.
Still, no one knows the back road we took to get here.

Where a disrupted heart becomes shattered glass for another
to sweep up.
The only problem is we keep cutting everyone that comes
close.

Bruised egos turn into chaos and chaos conforms a whole
being if left untreated.

These are the signs of a dislocation
and any woman that suffers from this injury must get medical
help immediately
except for a Black woman.

She's supposed to carry this pain around like a badge of
honor.
Tie absentee father and dead son around our necks like a
noose and still keep going.

Because let's face it, she's been losing parts of herself since
creation.
Starting with
her family,
her home,
her voice,
her wages,
her vagina,
her choices.
Even her physical attributes are snatchable.
We see others trademarking them as if they were their own.

Hold you hurt in Black girl.
Don't scream when you get molested.
Don't tell when your boss harasses you.
Don't go off when the doctor doesn't take your complaints
seriously.
Don't get angry when they touch your hair.
Don't "me too" if they touch you at all.
Don't cry!
Don't bend!
Don't break!
Stay strong!
We need you.

53

But I need me too.

This is how a Black girl grieves.
Don't give us pity.
Ask us why.

From left to right... my oldest sister Samoda, my mother Sabrina, myself, and my sister Sabria. We took this picture in front of Franklin Mills Mall back in the 90s.

I'm Sorry

To all the guys that told me I thought you were mean until I got to know you
I apologize for being me.

I'm sorry you couldn't see my dopeness firsthand or the way God sent his sunshine down to dance upon my cheeks.
I'm sorry that you couldn't see the light inside me because I swear that day I was beaming.

You see I left my home minding my business.
Covered in Almond Cookie, and good intentions.
Never did I envision you would see me as mean, rude, another vain Black woman with a chip on her shoulder.

We locked eyes,
I said a quick *hi* and kept it moving,
but I guess that wasn't good enough.

I'm sorry,
for coming into your presence without grinning on repeat as if by first glance I should have fallen to your feet and recited your name backward.

I'm sorry,
for sometimes having a face that says I don't take no shit and if you want to get to know me you might have to try a little bit.
This connection won't be easy.
.
I'm sorry,

that I don't smile for no reason.
Please stop telling me I need to.
Stop assuming because I'm pretty that life never knocks me off my feet.
Maybe sometimes my soul feels bruised and I just want to rock myself to sleep in a mood.

I'm sorry,
that where I'm from you have to build a tough exterior.
Lions pounce on lambs.
Sensitivity has no place on the streets of Philly, so you chase them down with a glass of grit.

A smile while walking past a group of guys in the middle of the night could get you rapped.
Because unfortunately, some men confuse my dimples for interest.
God forbid I say no thank you, then I have to be labeled a Bitch
as if there are no other words in a thirsty dude's vocabulary.

So I'm sorry,
that my hood got to me before you did.
Initially, I wasn't what you thought I should be.
However, what I am is cool, awkward,
an introvert with a soul-capturing heart,
that would rather kick it with a few good friends than a room full of strangers.

My quietness doesn't come from me being arrogant.
It comes from that gentle fear that creeps up inside of me whenever I have to mingle with the masses.

So I'm sorry,
That you didn't ask me how I was.
That you never took the time to see me before you prejudged.
That you settled for your assumptions instead of getting to know my authenticity.

And I'm sorry, I even had to write this poem
because dudes that jump to the conclusion without reading the book
are the ones that should be sorry.

Did you know that some of life's greatest gifts come in sealed packages, but it's up to you to unwrap them?

Take A Load Off

Your head on my shoulder feels heavier today.
Like a massive stone seeking rest from a pillow.

Allow my fullness to be your sanctuary.
Caress my soft edges and know that you are home.

You can surrender within my curves.
I offer only luxury and words that build.

The streets are hostile enough.
I am not your war.
I refuse to be your battle.

Light-Skinned Apologies

A Black girl,
in a colonized world,
offering light-skinned apologies.

Borrowed Dishes
(Dedicated to my sister Letrissa who passed away in 2018)

If time was a quote it would say the man that waits on me to pursue a dream is like a man that carries around luggage but goes on no trips.

If it had a sense of humor it would laugh every time we said I'll get to it later.

If it was a sermon the message would be about how often God extends grace,
but how it's never really reciprocated.

If time was a movie I would play the naive 30-something female, with natural hair, and her mother's freckles. Letrissa would play my sister from another mother.
The one that I got to choose.

During the opening scene, the camera would zoom into my face, and settle upon my stoic sadness.

The setting is Norfolk General.

The same hospital my classmate Darlene died in just a year prior.
It is there, in a cold sterilized hospital room
where the audience would catch me placing a kiss on my friends' forehead for the last time.

The next scene would be a flashback of the last 9 years.
Taking the viewers watching on a journey where I met this lotus flower on a Virginia Beach playground.
Side-eyed her smart mouth with sandbox appreciation.

Her Chi-town two-step connects to my Philly swing.
Flipping what looks like just another cohort into a sister.
Pour in a girl name Kim, and stir until you get
the purest three-way friendship you could have ever imagined.

Once teenage mothers talking about pre-teen issues.
Connecting over Israel Haughton and good Black men.
The audience watching would fall in love with these three modern-day girlfriends.

Nevertheless, in the last scene, you will witness how fragile time is.
How a second chance can quickly become the last one you get.
Three flowers that once bloomed together like spring,
now split like summer heartbreak.

I wish I would have known that sissy was growing weary.
That the person that everyone used for medicine wasn't strong enough

to heal herself.
I wish calling was more convenient than a text
and when we spoke I memorized her words backwards.
I wish I could have captured the songs she sang in my belly.
Hugged her tight enough to squeeze her aches away.

Nonetheless, time is fickle.
It can be your best friend or your worst enemy.
I wish I could tell you that this film is now playing in a theater near you,
but this isn't a movie, and in real life, I am reminded how time doesn't care about your fantastic new job, or that busy schedule you never seem to clock out of.

It doesn't care that your car is broken down
and you have no quick way to go visit your sick friend,
because she's in the hospital again.
That friend that holds all your secrets
is in the hospital again.

Time isn't fazed that you lose a little piece of yourself every time you see her in pain.
It doesn't blink when you pray for her mending.

Time simply demands that you prioritize between your girl and your errands.
That you make that taco Tuesday date.
That you find a way to take that girl's trip.
That you laugh and joke with her while watching the Super Bowl game even if your favorite team is playing because you might not ever get another opportunity to giggle with sis again.

This poem is not asking for your sympathy.
This poem wasn't written to make tears run down your cheeks.
This poem is not some desperate attempt to gain your snaps.

This poem is simply a reminder that the people we love are borrowed dishes.
Lent to us by God to be handled with care
until he comes to retrieve them.

Time doesn't care if you're not ready to let them go.
It's just hoping that death will teach us how to live.

From left to right...me, Kim and Letrissa.

Surrender

When I die,
bury my ashes along the shoreline
and allow the tide to wash me away,
so I can remember what it felt like to surrender.

The Wanderer

I call myself a wanderer
How do you have two homes and still come up missing?

Shifted from the city of brotherly love to Norfolk where the L is silent.
Been here for over a decade,
but still the streets don't hug me like a homie.

Can't get down with my broad street vernacular.
The way my water cuts too wavy.
The way I'll speak but won't reach too deep if you act like you don't hear me.

To some, I come off as arrogant.
Wearing this Eagles emblem on my chest like a trophy.
A daily reminder that I can fly here.
That I am *fly* here.

Rocking my sister's resting bitch face with a hint of *hey it's nice to meet you.*
It's hard to make new friends when nobody wants to greet you.
I hoped to create connections but it's not easy when they can't read you.

My parents are getting older,
living five hours away.

I can't move at the speed of lightning when they need me.

It's like trying to fit a square peg into a round hole. Sometimes it seems like I gotta sacrifice my sunny just to please them.

Back in Philly, I'm a bougie hood song over a country beat. What some dub conceit I call PA VA muscle.

I call myself a wanderer.
How do you have two homes and still come up missing?

Made in the USA
Columbia, SC
08 November 2023